D1711865

A DAY IN THE LIFE OF A
Seeing Eye® Dog Trainer

by Kevin Osborn
Photography by John Halpern

Troll Associates

Library of Congress Cataloging-in-Publication Data

Osborn, Kevin, (date)
    A day in the life of a seeing eye dog trainer / by Kevin Osborn;
photography by John Halpern.
        p.   cm.
    Summary: Describes the daily work of Pete Jackson, who trains dogs
to guide blind people and then teaches students how to work with
those dogs.
    ISBN 0-8167-2218-8 (lib. bdg.)   ISBN 0-8167-2219-6 (pbk.)
    1. Guide dogs—Training—Juvenile literature. 2. Guide dog
schools—Juvenile literature. [1. Guide dogs. 2. Dog trainers.
3. Occupations. 4. Jackson, Pete.] I. Halpern, John, 1957-   ill.
II. Title.
JV1780.2.083 1991
362.4′183—dc20   90-11076

The author and publisher would like to thank Michele Drolet, Pete Jackson, Doug
Roberts, Lori Scholz, and the Seeing Eye, Inc. for their generous assistance and
cooperation.

Seeing Eye® is a registered trademark for dog guides of the Seeing Eye, Inc.

Pete Jackson arrives at the Seeing Eye school at
7:45 in the morning. Pete trains dogs to guide blind
people, and then teaches students how to work with
those dogs. The first thing he has to do is serve
breakfast to the dogs at the kennel. The dogs live
there while he trains them.

After feeding his dogs, Pete plays with them in the kennel yard. Pete works with ten dogs at a time. He trains many different types of dogs: German shepherds, Labrador retrievers, golden retrievers, and some mixed breeds. Pete loves all his dogs, and they love him, too.

Each of Pete's dogs is one year old. Before being trained in guide work, Seeing Eye puppies spend a year living with families who belong to local 4-H clubs. These clubs help develop responsibility and leadership in young boys and girls through various programs, such as raising puppies. Ginger was the ninth puppy this family raised for the Seeing Eye.

At eight o'clock, Pete loads his dogs into a van and drives downtown to the Seeing Eye's training center. The dogs are eager to go to work, but they know they have to wait for Pete's command before getting into or out of the van.

While the other dogs wait in the van, Pete practices obedience training with Stoney. Stoney knows to walk beside him when Pete commands, "Heel!" He also obeys when Pete gives the command to come. It is important for Pete to praise Stoney whenever he does the right thing. "Good boy!" says Pete.

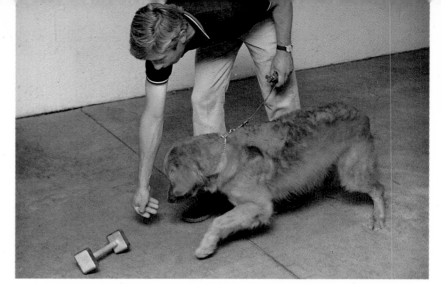

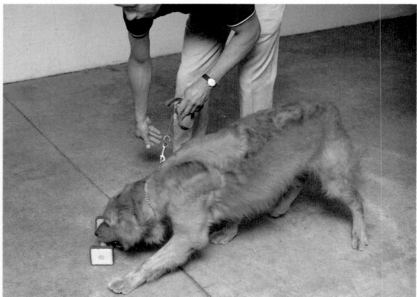

Next, Pete teaches Stoney how to retrieve dropped objects. After practicing with a fetch block, Pete will ask him to retrieve key chains, wallets, and gloves—things a blind person might drop. Like all dogs, Stoney wants to please human beings. So when he brings the block back, Pete praises and pets him.

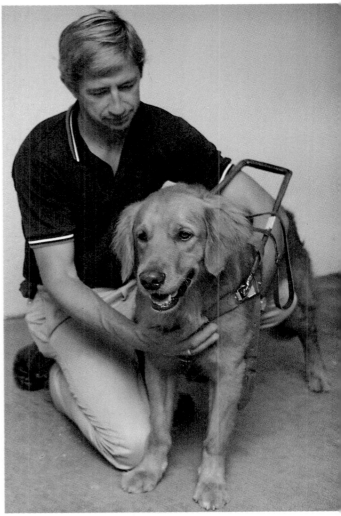

Pete grooms each dog every day. Grooming keeps
the dogs clean and helps show the dogs that Pete
cares for them. After Stoney has been groomed,
Pete puts a harness on him and works with him in
a variety of locations. Pete works outside with all
his dogs every day, rain or shine.

After Stoney has finished, it is Nitro's turn to work with Pete. First, Pete sets up a hurdle on the sidewalk. Then he pretends to be blind and orders Nitro to walk forward. When Nitro obeys his command, Pete bumps into the hurdle. Pete shouts, "Pfui!" as he slaps the hurdle with his hand. "Pfui" means "shame on you" in German, and it is used so the dogs know when they have made a mistake.

Pete repeats the exercise, ordering Nitro to move forward again. This time, Nitro disobeys his command. She leads Pete off the path and around the hurdle. Pete praises Nitro for learning what is called "intelligent disobedience." This means that Nitro refuses to obey a command that would put her owner in danger.

In "freelance" training, Pete introduces each dog to a variety of real-life situations. Pete has to hold Stoney back to teach him not to play with other dogs while he is on the job. Seeing Eye dogs cannot let other dogs, cats, or squirrels distract them from their work. They must concentrate on guiding their owners at all times.

In town, Pete approaches an awning that hangs just above his head. A week ago, Pete pretended to walk into this awning, slapped it, and shouted, "Pfui!" This time, Stoney steers him away from the awning. He has learned to protect Pete's head as well as his body from being bumped.

Pete wants to test Stoney's intelligent disobedience. He enters one of the town's busiest intersections and orders Stoney to cross into heavy traffic, but Stoney refuses to lead Pete into the path of an oncoming bus. Pete has taught Stoney to use his eyesight to judge danger and to disobey any dangerous commands.

When it is safe to cross the street, Stoney guides Pete to the other side. Stoney knows to avoid cars by a wide margin, just in case the driver is careless. As soon as they arrive safely at the opposite curb, Pete rewards Stoney for his intelligent disobedience. "Good dog!" he says, petting him.

After three months of training, Stoney is ready for the final test. Watched carefully by his supervisor, Pete wears a blindfold while Stoney guides him through town. Pete truly cannot see, but Stoney guides him well and passes the test. Once the test is complete, the 4-H family that raised Stoney is allowed to watch him from a distance for the last time before he is assigned to a blind student.

At 11:15, Pete drives back to the Seeing Eye kennel. After a full morning's work, Pete has a 45-minute play period with the dogs in the kennel yard, and he thinks about the blind students he will work with this afternoon. Although they have already started their program at the school, Pete recalls the day two weeks ago when the students first arrived.

On that Saturday morning, Pete welcomed Michele and other new students and led them to their rooms. Students live in these dorm rooms for one month. Pete walked through Michele's room, slapping the door, the dresser, the chairs, and the bed so Michele could hear where everything was. Pete also showed her where towels and linens were stored.

Pete then helped the students get to know the Seeing Eye facility. A special "map" is used that labels each room in "Braille"—a reading method used by blind people. Braille is read by using touch instead of sight. Patterns of raised bumps stand for different letters of the alphabet. By reading the Braille labels, Michele was able to find the location of the dining room.

On that Saturday afternoon Pete led each student on a "Juno walk." Juno is the name that the trainers use for an imaginary dog. Pete played the part of the "dog" by pulling the harness as a dog would. The Juno walk helped Pete learn the student's size, strength, walking speed, and agility. This knowledge allowed him to give each student a dog that best matched that student's needs and abilities.

On Sunday Pete's students met their dogs for the first time. These dogs had already completed their training with Pete and were ready to begin working with blind students. Pete told Michele to sit, crouch, or kneel, so that she and her dog would be at the same level. Michele was very excited to meet her new dog, a German shepherd named Tessa.

The first thing Pete taught Michele was how to harness Tessa. Then he showed her how to groom her dog. Michele must groom Tessa every day. Grooming helps Michele get into the habit of caring for her dog daily. It also creates a bond between Michele and Tessa.

This afternoon Pete is taking his students and their dogs into town. There, students will learn to travel routes that the dogs already know. Pete watches as Michele steps into the Seeing Eye van. Then Michele calls Tessa to join her inside. Tessa has learned to wait for this command.

Pete supervises Michele and Tessa on one of their routes. When the sidewalk is blocked, Tessa turns toward the street and stops at the curb. Michele listens, decides that it is safe, and gives Tessa the command, "Forward." If Tessa does not see any danger, she leads her owner off the curb, around the object, and back up onto the sidewalk.

Pete also teaches Michele and Tessa how to move through wide open spaces with no sidewalks. Pete offers advice to students on their routes. Most important, he makes sure no harm comes to his students as they get used to working as a team with their dogs.

When Michele and Tessa get more comfortable with each other, Pete teaches them more difficult skills. Revolving doors provide very little space for a person and a dog. Michele enters the door first and pushes Tessa to the front to avoid getting the dog's tail caught in the door.

Pete watches over Michele and Tessa when they go to the train station. Tessa blocks Michele from getting too close to the edge of the platform. Then they practice going down the stairs from the train station. Pete suggests that Michele lean back slightly. This helps her keep her balance against Tessa's weight and forward motion.

Pete also works with his students indoors. He teaches them to walk through tight spaces like store aisles and the gaps between restaurant tables. Most stores and restaurants do not usually allow animals inside, but by law, dogs that guide blind people are permitted to enter.

As they head back toward the training center, Michele and Tessa run into a dangerous situation. A stranger who loves dogs suddenly reaches out to pet Tessa. Although this woman only wants to be friendly, she has distracted Tessa and put Michele in danger. Pete explains to the stranger that Tessa must give her full attention to Michele in order to take care of her.

At 4:30, after all the students have practiced routes with their dogs, everyone returns to the dorms. Students and their dogs relax and play until dinner. By working and playing together, the dogs and their owners become true friends. Pete eats dinner with the students and answers any questions they may have.

Relaxing after dinner, Pete tells the students how dogs think and behave. He also explains that the students can correct their dogs by either tugging on the leash or by scolding them. During this informal lesson, the dogs lie at their owners' feet.

In a normal workday, Pete spends about thirteen hours on the job and walks almost fifteen miles. By the end of the day he is exhausted, but he loves his job. He enjoys working with both dogs and people. Pete knows that the work he does helps blind people gain a new feeling of freedom, and he feels good about that.